Bombers Over
MERSEYSIDE

This was Merseyside's 'Finest Hour': The Authoritative Record of the blitz, 1940-1941

LIVERPOOL

DAILY POST AND ECHO LTD.

1943

Authorised Reprint published by Scouse Press Liverpool L8 3SB

1983

THE FIRST BOMBS ON LIVERPOOL.
Clearing debris at the L.M.S. Goods Station, Caryl Street.

FOREWORD

By

The Rt. Hon. The Earl of Derby
P.C., K.G., G.C.B., G.C.V.O., T.D.

I AM delighted to think that the authentic story of the bombing of Merseyside is being published, because I feel it is a step in the right direction in placing on permanent record the triumphant bravery with which the people of Merseyside answered the brutal call on their courage and steadfastness.

In addition, I am convinced that even now what took place here is not generally known and full credit has not therefore been given to the way in which the whole of this area stood up to its testing.

I believe that with the publication of this book the country will better be able to appreciate—what we who know Merseyside already realise—the way in which the ordeal was faced.

Nothing could have been more inspiring, and it is right that this bravery should become known more widely than it is known at the present time.

It will, I think, be sufficient for me to say that I hope this account will stand for all time as a testimony to the gallant way in which the attack was met and be an example to all parts of the country if they should unfortunately be subjected to a similar attack.

THE ATTACK ON THE CITY . . .
Firemen battle with the blitz in St. George's
Crescent, Liverpool.

. . . AND ON HOMES. Church Street,
Wallasey. A typical block of blitzed
property

THIS WAS YOUR VICTORY

By S. C. Leslie (Ministry of Home Security)
Author of 'Front Line'

THE Battle of Britain, some say, began on August 8th, with the first heavy attacks on shipping off the coast. Others put the date at August 10th, when fleets of German bombers first attacked the coast.

For Merseyside the Battle of Britain, and her own nine-month ordeal, began on August 9th. There had been previous alerts, and a few bombs, but the first casualty on Merseyside was at 12.30 a.m. on August 9th, when a string of bombs was dropped in Prenton. Twenty-four hours later a stick of seven high explosive bombs fell upon Wallasey, upon a railway embankment, upon streets and the mains beneath them, upon houses and the people within. In all, there were 32 casualties in this raid.

These were but the opening notes of the long symphony of battle, that swelled and widened until the climax, when it crashed and roared in the great May-time raids of the following year.

The picture of the blitz on Britain in 1940-41 has two faces. One is the picture of flame and craters, of rubble and broken bodies, of brave endurance and steady service in the little streets of cities.

The other is a pattern of strategy, of total attack and defence, essential parts of a struggle that even then raged in two continents, five oceans, and the skies above them all.

At first, the Mersey Boroughs played little part in this strategy. The German Air Force, in August, was striking as the R.A.F. struck at Sicily before the Allied landing, to crush defensive power and open the way for the invasion barges. In September came the great attempt to batter London into inactivity or submission. With its failure, in October, the thoughts of the German High Command turned from the hope of easy and immediate triumph to the certainty of a

longer struggle. Britain would not compromise, and she knew how to parry and beat back the attempt at a Knock-out in Round One. She would fight on, and with every month that passed her unreadiness would more and more be made good and her fighting strength would grow. So the roots of that strength must be cut : the war factories must be bombed and the arms workers scattered and demoralised. And late in October, and in November, this phase of the attack began, reaching its first climax with the historic attack on Coventry on November 14th.

But Britain's strength did not come from her war factories alone. As the prospect and

The Liver Bird's narrow escape.

perspective of war lengthened, the Empire's strength was increasingly mobilised ; the United States realised that the hope of successful resistance to Hitler in Europe was not dead, and quickened her efforts to help ; the neutral countries' resources were tapped by trade. Across the seas of the world, from every free land, flowed an increasing stream of weapons and munitions of war, of raw materials and food. Under the Navy's guns, it made its way to the advanced striking base of Freedom. It reached the factories and shops, the houses and camps of Britain—through her great ports. Here then was the next target. And here remained the chief target for the Luftwaffe, for as long as it was free to undertake independent operations.

This attack upon the ports of Britain was a major operation of war. The intention was as large, the significance as wide, the hope perhaps as great, as those of to-day's great combined bombing offensive on Germany. The scale was smaller, and the result was very different—but that is not the point.

The Civil Defenders and the citizens of British ports in the months from November to May of 1940-41 were defeating a blockade that, if successful, would have ended the war. They were fighting a battle—one of the decisive battles of history. The Mersey towns combine to make what was, for the war-time purposes of those years, the greatest port in Britain. To keep it open was vital. It was kept open, and working. That is the sum of its citizens' achievement.

. . . . .

Following the first attacks on Birkenhead and Wallasey there came the first stick of bombs on Liverpool, in the night of August 17th-18th. Ten days later, on the night of August 28th, came another small attack on Liverpool. The same thing happened the following night : and the night after that—Wallasey getting the bombs this time. On the next night again, the last of the month, there came a comparatively heavy attack, in which Liverpool, Birkenhead and Wallasey were all hit. Casualties were the highest up to that date.

In Liverpool alone there were over 100 fires—mostly, of course, small. The Custom House, Wallasey Town Hall, and a

Henry Street, Birkenhead.

Pool Bank, Port Sunlight.

Wellington Road, Liverpool.

LINE WAS IN YOUR STREET

Wallasey Road, Wallasey.

Boundary Road, Port Sunlight.

Guffitt's Rake, Meols.

Ballantyne Road, West Derby.

Brassey Street, Birkenhead.

Wesley Street, Waterloo.

number of houses, shops and offices, were hit.

That was the real beginning of what was to prove a very lively three months. There were actually twenty light raids on Merseyside in September, fifteen in October, and nine in November—forty-four, or an average of one almost every other night. Of the twenty raids in September, Liverpool had bombs sixteen times, Birkenhead eleven times, Bootle nine times, Wallasey nine times, and Crosby four times.

In October's fifteen raids, Liverpool escaped only once, while Birkenhead was hit seven, Bootle six, and Wallasey three times. Liverpool was a target in every raid in November, and the Mersey boroughs had their fair share.

While many of these raids were small and some of them almost wholly ineffective, the accumulation of them made a considerable impact on the daily—or nightly—lives of many citizens, especially those who lived nearest the docks on either side of the estuary. There began at this time that poignant late-afternoon trek of mothers and children to the shelters, with father sometimes joining them after work to make sure of a good night's rest and a good day's work next day. Merseyside was getting used to the idea that it was in the front line.

On September 6th, a Children's Convalescent Home was hit in Birkenhead—happily without fatal result. During September there were a number of what nowadays we might call " sharp " raids on Merseyside. The Central Station, Liverpool, was hit, and coaching stock damaged, on the night of September 21st-22nd. Five nights later there was a substantial fire raid on the docks and warehouses ; at one dock there was a big fire that still " showed a light " the following evening. Two theatres were set alight, one of which was the world-famous Argyle Theatre, Birkenhead, which was gutted.

The raids of October and November did not again extend the fire or civil defence services to the same extent until the night of November 28th-29th. This was Merseyside's real baptism of fire, the first full scale attack on the port, and only the second major stroke in the air blockade. (The first was the medium-sized attack on Southampton on November 23rd.)

At 7.23 p.m. on November 28th, the Liverpool sirens sounded, and before long the citizens had cause to realise that an attack was in progress greater than they had known—something on the scale of the big attacks on the arms towns of which they had read. A load of explosive and incendiary bombs, heavy by the reckoning of those days, fell steadily over the city and many points outside it. The main weight of attack lasted $2\frac{1}{2}$ hours, until ten o'clock. In that short time more than 200 people were killed in the whole area—a very grievous blow.

On the following night a few scattered bombs fell about Edge Hill Station, but after that Merseyside was left in peace for three weeks, until December, when the " Christmas raids " brought the next great instalment of battle to the estuary and its people.

The first raid, on December 20th, began at half-past six. Bombs were falling from that hour until four the following morning. The first hour and a half was comparatively quiet, but from eight o'clock until eleven the raid was at its height. There was soon a fire situation which over-taxed the resources of the local services and called into being a reinforcement scheme from a wide area.

Food warehouses in Dublin Street and the Waterloo Grain House were alight, and there were some notable fires in the docks, while smaller ones burned at civic buildings, the Cunard Buildings and the Dock Board Offices. Exchange Station was closed, and for a time all lines out of it were stopped.

Both in Liverpool and in Bootle there was a good deal of damage to houses. In Liverpool, a bomb which had penetrated the ground below two shelters exploded, pinning many of the occupants against the roof. Magnificent rescue work brought out 48 people, but 42 lives were lost.

A series of five railway arches in Bentinck Street, Liverpool, used as an unofficial shelter and crowded with people, were directly hit. This was one of the most dreadful of the night's incidents. The arches were quite destroyed, collapsing in huge concrete blocks and showers of ballast on to the packed ground

BOOTLE HAVOC.—There were 25,000 homeless in the May blitz. Here is a scene only too often repeated throughout the Borough.

beneath. The work of rescue was exceptionally difficult, since the blocks of concrete could not be moved, and were hard enough to turn the chisels of the compressors brought up to split them. After many days, when the work was complete, 42 bodies had been extricated.

Next night the advance guards of an even bigger raiding force made their appearance at almost the same time as before, and loosed a rain of fire and high explosive bombs which lasted until five in the morning. The weight of the attack came in two waves—from about seven o'clock until ten-thirty, and then from about midnight until half-past three. The raid was an even bigger and more serious affair than that of the preceding night. The docks, particularly the northern part, were hit repeatedly. Warehouses were set on fire, and, in the centre of the city, St. George's Hall was damaged badly. There was a fairly long list of serious fires.

Hundreds of houses were struck, especially in the Anfield district, and a direct hit on a large shelter caused the worst single tragedy of the night. When the rescue service and the searchers had completed their work there, 74 bodies in all had been brought out for burial.

The raid spread its effects over Bootle, Birkenhead, Seaforth and Wallasey, with minor incidents elsewhere, but the main burden of the blow was borne by Liverpool itself. The civil defence services everywhere stood up to their greatest test in a way that fully satisfied their leaders. They had all they could do to cope with the succession of calls that rained in on them, but they managed to do it. The after-raid problem of housing and feeding the homeless also made heavy demands on those responsible, and heroic work brought much relief.

Among the buildings damaged were the Mill Road Infirmary, the Gaiety Cinema,

St. Anthony's School, Crescent Church and St. Alphonsus' Church. Exchange Station was closed and a number of railway lines were out of action for a short time. December 23rd was Manchester's night, and the Mersey towns had but a light attack, in comparison with the earlier two, though Birkenhead dockside warehouses were badly damaged and many fires were started. On these three nights, 356 men, women and children, lost their lives, and the area took its place alongside those others which had experienced the worst horrors that air bombardment could at that time inflict. Wallasey alone suffered 119 fatalities, 13 of the victims being elderly inmates of a Widows' Home, who were gassed by the broken mains while trapped under the debris of the bombed building.

. . . . . .

After the turn of the year, attacks over the whole country slackened for a time. There were three raids about the Mersey in the first ten days of January, followed by more than a month of peace and quiet. February saw two raids, on the 15th and 24th. Then, a fortnight later, came another heavy attack. About nine o'clock on the evening of March 12th, flares were dropped all over the Merseyside area. The bombs soon followed and lasted until three in the morning. The main weight of attack fell upon the docks, more especially on the Cheshire side, and there was considerable damage to houses both in Birkenhead and Wallasey ; indeed, these two boroughs had reason to consider March 12th as " their " raid, though Liverpool itself by no means entirely escaped. This was Wallasey's worst experience of all, the bombing being widespread and the total number of deaths was more than half the total of 328 for the whole nine months " blitz " period of 1940-41.

In Wallasey a few lucky hits interrupted water, gas and electricity services for some days. In Birkenhead the General Hospital had to be evacuated. Birkenhead reported a great number of fires, the majority of them fortunately small, and the Borough had 288 killed in that month as a whole, mostly in the March 12th raid. It is worth noting that in that month Liverpool itself lost 101 citizens killed, so that the com-

parative severity of the blow to the Cheshire boroughs can easily be seen.

There were lighter attacks on Merseyside on the following evening, March 13th, and again as it happened, Birkenhead and Wallasey had the worst of it, but the whole scale of events was very much smaller and the renewal of attack hardly slowed up the work of repair and rehabilitation that was going forward. Again, the next evening, there were raiders over the Mersey ; some high explosive fell in Liverpool, and some incendiaries in Birkenhead and Wallasey, but the effects were negligible. For the time being the blow was over.

It was on the morrow of these raids that one of the strangest episodes of all blitzed Britain took place. On Sunday morning, March 16th, a rescue party working in Lancaster Avenue, Wallasey, heard what they thought was a kitten's faint mew below them in the debris. Listening in silence they heard it again—it was a baby's cry. Getting feverishly to work the three men made their way towards where a child of a few months was lying buried, and half choked with dust. Moving like cats themselves, lest one ill-judged gesture should loose a pile of debris on to the child, they finally reached it, gave it first aid, wiped the dust from its mouth and released it. The child had lain there $3\frac{1}{2}$ days, from the time the bomb exploded in the early morning of the fateful March 12th to the moment of its rescue—almost incredible, but true. The rescued child is today, three years later, a handsome smiling girl and is in the care of her maternal grandparents, both her father and mother having been killed in the " blitz." She is by way of being an heiress, a sum of £844 being held in trust for her. A tin containing £350 and a cash-box with securities were found among the wreckage, while a considerable sum was due to the father by way of superannuation contributions as a Dock Board employee.

There were three more raids before the end of April, on the 7th a very slight affair, on the 15th a sharper attack, and on the 26th a widely spread and not very effective attack over the whole area. Casualties were light, and incendiary bombs were very quickly smothered by the new Fire Guard

The Battle of the Docks: A Seacombe Mill which came into the line of fire.

that was now beginning to find its feet and show the result of its organisation and practice.

. . . . .

In March and April the Luftwaffe was increasing the tempo and weight of its attack on British ports. On March 10th, Portsmouth was heavily attacked ; on March 12th, Merseyside ; on the two following nights there were big attacks on Clydeside ; on March 18th, Hull was the target ; on March 20th and 21st, Plymouth. In April, Portsmouth (10th), Belfast (15th), and Plymouth (21st, 22nd, 23rd, 27th and 28th) were heavily hit. The enemy was moving quickly towards the climax of his onslaught.

Looking back in the light of later events we know that he intended withdrawing his Air Force about the middle of May in preparation for the attack on Russia five or six weeks later, and that he planned as a parting shot to do the utmost possible harm

to this, one of the most vital spots in Britain. This part of his plan was clearly of importance to him ; though he must have known he would have need of all the aeroplanes he could muster for the attack in Eastern Europe, he did not hesitate to send them out over Britain in full force, and to accept losses on a rapidly growing scale, culminating in the destruction of 160 of his planes in the first half of May.

Assuming that he hoped to complete his overthrow of Russia by the end of the year, it is reasonable to suppose that to put the port of Liverpool out of action for many weeks, if he could have achieved it, would have seemed to him an objective well worthy of attaining. By interrupting the flow of supplies from the west, this might have slowed up Britain's defensive and offensive preparations enough to make a substantial difference when the time came for the Germans to turn their back on prostrate Russia and, as they calculated, finish the

'WIDE OPEN SPACES.'—Above shows the devastated area in Borough Road, Birkenhead, and (below) the equally awesome scene in the Rimrose Road area of Bootle.

war by all-out attack on the last defiant opponent.

It is against this background that the May-time raids on Merseyside must be considered. They continued, as is well known, for eight successive nights—the first eight nights of the month. It will help to gain a picture of the course of that violent and desperate week if some general facts about it are set out briefly.

The first night was a comparatively light attack. There were rather less than a hundred incidents in Liverpool, and none in Bootle—the two Boroughs which bore by far the greatest part of the week's attack, but there were casualties caused also in a suburban area in Birkenhead. On the following night the scale nearly doubled. The third night saw a heavy and continuous attack—the heaviest of the whole week, with six or seven hundred incidents in Liverpool and in Bootle, and a fire situation of great seriousness in both boroughs.

On May 4th, 5th and 6th, the attacks were of moderate weight. The attack on the night of May 7th was again a savage one, with around 300 incidents in the two boroughs, and again an extensive and serious fire situation in the Docks and City. Much damage was done to property at New Brighton in the early hours of May 8th, and it was there that the ferry steamer " Royal Daffodil II " was sunk at her moorings at Seacombe landing stage. The next night, May 8th, saw some scattered raiding and few incidents.

The raids were of varying duration. The first lasted for about 2½ hours, from shortly before 11 o'clock ; the second for nearly 4 hours, from about 10.45 ; the third from about 11 to 3.30 ; the fourth from about 1 till 4 in the morning ; the fifth from about 20 past midnight to about 4.15 ; the 6th from 12.30 to 4 o'clock ; the 7th began about the same time and lasted a little longer.

The weight and severity of the attack can best be judged from a few figures. In Liverpool, for instance, the killed numbered more than 1,400 and there were more than 1,000 seriously injured. In Liverpool, Bootle and the adjoining fringe of Litherland and Crosby, nearly 90,000 houses were destroyed or damaged to some extent. This total represented about 40 per cent. of all the houses in the area concerned. In Bootle, which had the greatest weight of attack, about 80 per cent. of the houses were affected in some degree by bombs or blast or fire. Birkenhead's dwellings also suffered severely as, out of a total of about 34,000, over 25,000 were damaged. Over 1,600 were hit as many as three times. In Wallasey, no fewer than 7,500 persons had to be evacuated, owing to damage to their homes.

On two nights the Fire Services were very heavily taxed by the immense concentration of flame in the centre of the City and in the Docks. On the night of May 3-4th, there were several hundred fires, needing the attendance of pumps—one of the heaviest tasks in relation to the area affected which any Fire Service had to face anywhere during the great raids of 1940-41.

While the number of fires on the second of the heavy nights, May 7th, was not so great, the situation confronting the Fire Service was in some respects worse. Roads and services had deteriorated in the meantime, there was more interruption of water supplies, and the weariness of the fire fighting men themselves was greater.

From Seaforth to Huskisson Dock the flames raged and burned, in ships, in warehouses and in the dockside sheds. The men who fought those fires had to work not only under a steady fall of bombs released all along the line of the docks but amid the extra hazards of the shot and shell surrounding them in the quay sheds and the holds of ships. The deeds of splendid heroism that were lost in the chaos of those nights' work will, many of them, never be known, but the accident of circumstances has brought some of them to light.

One of the war's most striking examples of civilian heroism occurred when, during a heavy raid on Liverpool in the May " blitz " of 1941, a number of railwaymen employed by the L.M.S. took their lives in their hands, and showed great courage and determination when an enemy bomb hit an ammunition train at Clubmoor and set it on fire. Wagon after wagon blew up, but with complete indifference to danger, the men uncoupled the rear section of the train before the flames had reached it and shunted it away before greater disaster could follow, for the wagons detached, it was stated, were laden with sea mines. One of the men, who had rushed from his home nearby to help, continued uncoupling wagons in spite of repeated explosions amid the ammunition on the train and the bursts of bombs, and another returned to his signal-box after being blown from it by an explosion.

The fate of one munition ship is known. She was berthed in Huskisson Dock. Her story, and the story of the men who fought to save her, can be told in these hitherto unpublished extracts from the letter sent by her master to the Fire Service Authorities.

" Dear Sir,

Amongst the general cargo the '————' was carrying were 1,000 tons of H.E. bombs. These were stored in numbers 1, 3 and 6 hatches, and at approximately 11.15 p.m. on May 3rd, 1941, some short time after the air-raid warning siren had sounded, and where there was a great deal of air activity going on, a partly inflated barrage balloon fell on the for'ard deck of my ship, over No. 1 hatch, and started to blaze fiercely ; pumps were got to work, and in 15 minutes the fire was put out by members of the crew. While the engagement with the burning balloon was taking place, a shower of incendiaries, and several H.E. bombs fell on the neighbouring dock sheds ; some incendiaries also fell on the deck of the '————'; these were successfully dealt with.

Around midnight, the shed on the East side was utterly demolished and the ruins blazing

These gaunt walls of Ranleigh Road, off Edge Lane, Liverpool, tell their own grim story.

fiercely, the shed on the South side was also violently ablaze, and it appeared that the water played on it for quenching purposes, only intensified the flames when it contacted the goods stored inside ; the whole shed soon became a raging inferno, and the flames from it spread to the '————' enveloping the ship from stem to stern. It soon became apparent that the flames were fast becoming too strong for our meagre fire appliances ; the heat, too, was proving overpowering to the men, so I gave orders to abandon ship.

We left via the ship's gangway and made a way along the quayside to a point where the shed was least affected by fire.

Immediately, I contacted the nearest Auxiliary Fire Station, which was situated at North-West Huskisson No. 1, but I found it unattended, as all personnel were engaged fire fighting at the adjacent dock sheds ; I went over to them, found the Officer in Charge, i.e., John Lappin, and acquainted him with the state of the fire on board my ship, and also of the dangerous cargo she carried ; Lappin immediately 'phoned from his station to his Headquarters, and asked for assistance, stating the facts as I had given them. After this, he employed all available hands of the '————' to work on the fire along with his own men, and his patience and tenacity as a leader aroused the admiration of all who witnessed it. He had little equipment, insufficient men, the scene of the fire was a continuous target for the enemy bombers which seemed to ceaselessly dive-bomb over us, yet he pursued his arduous task unflinchingly, and the men at his command, with admirable courage, carried out his instructions.

I realised the danger of the men, who, led by Lappin, continued their endeavour to penetrate the blazing wall of shed fires to reach the ship ; several times I put the dangerous situation to Lappin, but although he and his men knew well the extent of their danger, they would not be deterred, Lappin replying that such risks were demanded of the fire services.

Around 3 a.m., Lappin decided to go personally to acquaint the Chief Officer of the Fire Brigade with the facts of the situation, and the urgency of the assistance he had requested by 'phone. I accompanied him and along with him spoke to Chief Officer Owen, who agreed to send a special tender with oxy-acetylene burning apparatus, to enable us to cut a hole in the port side of the ship in the hopes of scuttling her.

We returned to the scene of fire and the promised tender duly arrived, but the ship exploded before anyone could approach to sink her.

Several men were injured when the explosion took place, myself included, and I regret to have to state that lives were lost.

(Signed) H. C. KINLEY."

On that same night there were grim and strenuous scenes enacted outside the Docks as well as in them. One of the most terrible of the night's episodes followed upon the fall of an exceptionally heavy bomb in the back courtyard of Mill Road Infirmary. It completely demolished three large hospital buildings and damaged all the rest of the hospital and the houses about it. Many people, patients and others, were trapped by debris, and to add to the horror of the scene and the difficulty of the task, fire broke out among the ambulances and cars assembled in the courtyard. Doctors, nurses and helpers specially summoned worked steadily among conditions of appalling difficulty to get the injured away and to release the trapped.

All the patients were transferred to other hospitals. One of them was actually on the operating table in an underground emergency theatre when the catastrophe occurred. He was buried amid debris and an attendant nurse was trapped beneath. After many hours of hard work a volunteer rescue party saved them both.

While this work of salvage and rescue was continuing H.E. and incendiary bombs were falling nearby, while at a factory less than 100 yards distant a large fire burned to add to the sense of menace and to act as a magnet for enemy bombs. In the Mill Road Hospital disaster, 17 members of staff, 15 ambulance drivers and some 30 patients lost their lives, while 70 people were seriously injured; 380 patients were transferred safely to other hospitals.

The Civil Defence Service themselves suffered relatively heavy casualties during the week. Of the wardens and W.V.S., 28 were killed and 14 injured ; 11 police were killed and 51 injured ; 27 of the casualty services lost their lives, and 6 were seriously injured ; 5 rescue men were killed and 5 injured.

The public buildings destroyed or damaged included Liverpool's Head Post Office, the Central and Bank Exchanges, the Mersey Dock Offices, the George Dock Buildings, the Oceanic Buildings, the India Buildings, the Corn Exchange, the Public Library and the Museum, and much destruction to many

THREE ESCAPE STORIES.—He came out of this house uninjured! (Below)—A near miss at Birkenhead.

The occupant walked out of the house (picture below) and saw it collapse like this.

churches, including St. Nicholas' Parish Church and St. Luke's Church.

Destruction of houses on the scale that has been indicated meant that the Civic Authorities had to deal with an enormous number of homeless people. In Liverpool alone the total was 51,000. In Bootle, where the destruction was proportionately far greater, there were 25,000 homeless, and the problem was further aggravated by the fact that more than three-quarters of the Rest Centre accommodation had been put out of action. Towards the end of the week billeting inside the Borough became out of the question, and special emergency measures had to be taken to billet people at short notice in reception towns at various distances from the Borough boundaries. The work was done very rapidly. By May 9th, over 10,000 had thus been housed and special transport arranged for the men who were coming in to work on Merseyside.

Besides those whose homes had been destroyed or damaged beyond use, there was a large number of people who, after the first three or four nights of attack, began to move out each afternoon from the hardest-hit Dockside neighbourhoods to seek a quiet night's rest and comparative safety a little further out. This extract from an eyewitness's letter will give the spirit and atmosphere of those strange, catastrophic, heroic days :—

"The people have been wonderful. Some of the sights, though sad, have been awe-inspiring. We have had extra police from counties and villages miles around, they have been brought in by special 'buses, and when seen, the people have cheered at them and the poor men all they could do was to look sheepish and grin. There are masses of Army lorries, mobile canteens and American canteens as well. One canteen round us is from Charlotteville, U.S.A. At night, lorry after lorry goes down our road (the only one open at all), with men, women and children, with blankets and pillows, etc. They are taking them up into Huyton Woods to sleep—but they are laughing and cheering the whole time—wonderful people.

In the evening you see queues and queues of men, women and children waiting to be taken away. One lorry comes up, they get in, in perfect order, no pushing ; as each one gets in they give their name and a special permit card to an officer and then get driven away. The orderliness and the quiet way it's done is wonderful, but very sad when you watch them."

At the peak of raiding, on the last night, the number of those officially known to have been accommodated outside in this way, was about 50,000—not as many as those actually rendered homeless. Though there must have been many more who made their own arrangements and did not figure in any official record, the total number affected was after all not a very great proportion of the population. The men came back daily in numbers as large as were needed to keep the Port working. The last and essential word on this aspect of the May-time raids is that at no time after the blitz was the working of the Docks restricted by lack of labour.

That brings us to the heart of the matter. At the end of the week of trial and terror, the enemy's main objective was unrealised. The great Mersey artery was not unaffected by this all-out blitz. Ships were damaged ; ships were sunk ; ships were diverted, some of them, to other ports ; sheds and their contents were destroyed ; dock communications were interrupted, gates and basins were hit, quaysides were struck. Yet when all was done a very substantial proportion of the Dock system was in action, while with every subsequent day that passed the return to normal progressed and accelerated.

The May-time attacks can fairly be reckoned a major engagement in the Battle of the Atlantic. The result was a genuine British victory. For this defensive achievement the citizens of Merseyside and the Civil Defence Services, who had for one week endured in full and literal measure blood, toil, tears and sweat, can claim a great share of the glory. By skill and endurance, by obstinate courage and organising capacity, they kept themselves and their community alive and working. Every member of the Civil Defence Services has the right to regard the outcome of the May-time raids as in some sense his or her personal achievement. Whether warden or ambulance driver, rescue worker or W.V.S. cook, fireman or first-aid member, each one can look back on May week of 1941 and say :—

"*That was my battle. I helped to win that victory. When Britain still stood alone, and the enemy struck at her most savagely, I had my chance to help the country keep fighting— and I took it.*"

Unforgettable Pictures

Sixteen pages of Memorable photographs

THIS WAS ONCE THEIR HOME—NOW IT IS A BATTLEFIELD.

THE ATTACK ON CULTURE. The gutted
City Museum, a victim of Nazi Vandalism.

SENSELESS DESTRUCTION at the University.
This was the Engineering Department.

Luftwaffe Target—Mill Road Hospital, Liverpool.

South Castle Street after a week of raids.

'Roman Bath'
Reflections.

❖

Cook Street
Arcade (above)
burning after the
1941 'fire blitz'
and as it is to-day
—an emergency
reservoir.

❖

**BUSINESS
AS USUAL.**

❖

Typical of the
'carry-on' spirit
on Merseyside
were these business
men who, blitzed
out of their offices,
continued to trans-
act business in the
streets.

**Only the Main Entrance remained of the
Liverpool Corn Exchange.**

WALLASEY TOWN HALL.
The wrecked organ.

THE BATTLE

'Measured by the weight and number of attacks, and number of
casualties, Merseyside was Hitler's Target Number One outside
London '—this was the official summing up of the 1940-41 blitz.
Here, in one mighty panorama of havoc, is what remained of the
once proud and imposing thoroughfares, Lord Street, and South

MERSEYSIDE.

Castle Street, in the heart of Liverpool. Here, too, in one picture,
is epitomised the ordeal—and the glory—of Merseyside, for it was
spectacles of destruction, such as this, that steeled the Merseysiders'
resolution to defeat the Luftwaffe's brazen challenge.

. . . and to-day, we give it back.

THE BATTLE LINE HOLDS.

All that remained of Bryant & May's Factory at Bootle.

'Main Street War.' Firemen battle with blazing buildings in Church Street.

Ranelagh Street, Liverpool, covered in debris from buildings on both sides.

TO HIT BACK.
Clearing a Lord Street area to obtain salvage.

ZERO HOUR.   An impressive night study made by the blazing L.M.S. Waterloo Goods Station.

A gutted car storage depot.

A blaze was seen for miles from this wrecked gas-holder at Linacre.

A BLITZ PATTERN. Another Liverpool street memory was this Church Street shop façade.

SYMBOL of Merseyside's invincible patriotism. Mrs. Reilly, whose husband was killed when their home was bombed, presents a bouquet to the Queen.

Dawn breaks in Virgil Street, Liverpool.

MERSEYSIDE'S CIVIL DEFENCE SERVICES GO INTO ACTION

By Hartley Shawcross, K.C.

(NORTH-WEST REGIONAL COMMISSIONER)

UNTIL the throb of their engines had actually followed close upon the wailing of the air-raid sirens there were not a few complacent people who thought that there would never be Bombers over Merseyside. " It won't happen," they used to say, easily. This of the war itself. And—when war came —"they can't get over the Pennines." But there were others who, mindful of their responsibility as citizens, enrolled in the Civil Defence Services of the Merseyside Area from the end of 1937 onwards.

Merseyside owes much to those who were serving when war came.

With the war, many of the existing part-time volunteers became whole-time members of their various services and large numbers of additional men and women enrolled. They were, as they are now, people of all types, all classes, and all ages, joined together in a common determination to stand firm against whatever danger and whatever terror might come.

In each town the Services were operated under the direction of a Controller—in Liverpool, Birkenhead, and Bootle the Town Clerk, in Wallasey the Chief Constable ; in Litherland, Waterloo and Crosby the Clerk to the Lancashire County Council ; at Bebington the Chief Constable of Cheshire. Within the group mutual assistance was organised and, as far as possible, coordination achieved through the Town Clerk of Liverpool as Group Controller.

For a long time nothing came. Those were the months of what was called the " phoney war." Months during which Merseyside was helping to strengthen the defences and to build up the resources of the country and, in Civil Defence, training and organising—and standing by. But then came the invasion of Holland and Belgium ; the bombing of Rotterdam, the collapse of France. There

was a new sense of urgency ; more people enrolled in the Civil Defence Services. Training was intensified ; added precautions were taken. But Spring turned into High Summer and still there were no Bombers over Merseyside.

It was not until the 25th June, 1940, that the first Air Raid Alert was sounded, and the heavy double-noted throb of the enemy aircraft, so reminiscent of the Gothas of the last war, was heard from behind a clouded sky. People went to their dug-outs and shelters. The Civil Defence personnel dashed to their action stations. All were ready for whatever might come. But still nothing came. There were no bombs, no guns. And presently the drone of the engines died away. The first bombs came on the night of July 28-29. Three of them, near a searchlight post at Altcar. Then followed a period of spasmodic raids and the first relatively big attack on Merseyside on August 31st. From that time till the end of November, raiding was almost continuous. On the 6th September, the Cathedral sustained some damage by blast ; some of its beautiful stained glass was destroyed. But then and throughout the black winter and the blacker spring which followed, the structure was unharmed and, at dawn, from down the river and from across it, it still stood, stark and upright against the horizon, at once a landmark and a symbol.

During all these raids, Merseyside carried on. There were many casualties ; there was much damage. But day after day the people, often a little weary, their eyes perhaps a little heavy with lack of sleep, turned out to their jobs. The factories still hummed with activity ; the shops opened in a sometimes pathetic and often gallant determination to carry on business as usual.

Night after night, often after a hard day's work, the Civil Defence personnel stood to

Firefighters in action, Whitechapel, Liverpool.

their posts. Many were wounded; many were killed. At Wallasey, for instance, on the 17th September, a bomb striking an A.F.S. post killed eight members of the A.F.S. on duty inside it.

But the Civil Defence personnel of Merseyside knew that Britain stood alone against the enemy and they were proudly conscious of the fact that they held what was a vital part of Britain's front line of battle. They held it well.

On the night of the 28th November, some hundreds of high explosive bombs were dropped. The guns of Merseyside fought back fiercely. None the less, the damage was severe. From just after 7 o'clock in the evening until 4 o'clock in the morning, almost without pause, the attack continued.

Outside the Junior Technical School at Durning Road, two tramcars, full of people, stopped at the height of the raid in order that their occupants might take cover in a public shelter under the school. A few minutes later bombs brought down the heavy solid building. The horror was added to by fire breaking out in the debris. Sixty of those trapped were rescued alive, but 180 others were killed in that " incident " alone.

There were many deeds of gallantry that night, countless quiet deeds of heroism which escaped official recognition but which live brightly in the hearts of those who witnessed them.

For three weeks Merseyside was free from heavy attack and then, on the 20th, 21st and 22nd December, came three seemingly interminable nights in which each raid was longer than the one preceding it. For ten hours, for eleven and then for twelve, the people waited and the Civil Defence Services fought before the steady note of the siren brought relief. There was heavy damage and again there were incidents in which shelters were hit and large numbers of people were killed.

The Rescue Services worked with great energy and saved many lives. The fire brigades had a heavy task. The Germans did not lie when they said the glow of fires could be seen for miles.

The Wardens, as always the backbone of Civil Defence, helping in fire-fighting, in rescue work, in first-aid, carrying out the manifold other duties they are called upon to perform, brought help to countless people and stiffened the morale of the whole population.

The women of the W.V.S., quietly going about their work, gave food and comfort to the homeless. Whilst the bombs were still falling, the ordinary, simple, diffident, often nervous women of the W.V.S. worked on, bringing new hope and fresh courage to those who had borne the battle.

St. George's Hall, the Assize Courts, was set on fire. Thousands of Law Reports contributed to the flames, more illuminating perhaps than they had ever been before. It mattered little. But underneath many hundreds of people were in shelters now in grave danger of collapse. That mattered much. At the very peak of the raid they had to be transferred and shepherded by the Wardens and the Police to other shelters.

Nearby, in Roe Street, a fire engine urgently responding to a call, was driven into a crater in the road. All of its crew of seven were killed.

Bootle, Litherland and Crosby, Birkenhead and Wallasey, also suffered severely. There was considerable damage at the Docks. A delayed action bomb burst the banks of the Leeds-Liverpool Canal. A steel barge,

carried through the breach, came to rest in the Railway Yard.

On the 23rd December, Merseyside breathed again. The fires were gradually subdued ; the homeless accommodated ; the life of the great area slowly restored.

There were more alerts, more raids, but it was not until ten weeks later that the district was again to be the subject of heavy attack. In the meantime much had been done ; the lessons, and there were many, taught by the bitter experience, were applied.

Then came the nights of the 12th, 13th and 14th March, 1941. This time, whether by design or, more probably, by miscalculation in the first instance, it was the Cheshire side of the river which bore the brunt of the attack.

Tens of thousands of incendiary bombs, and hundreds of high explosive bombs, fell on Bebington, Birkenhead and Wallasey.

In Wallasey, within less than two hours of the first attack, the water supplies for fire-fighting failed completely, the trunk main having been fractured by a bomb.

A large number of fires were attended in the course of this raid and the Regional Authorities brought in firemen collected from 39 cities and towns in Lancashire, Cheshire, and North Wales. And so with

FRONT LINE STRETCHER. —Civil Defence workers face the bombs to bring in the injured.

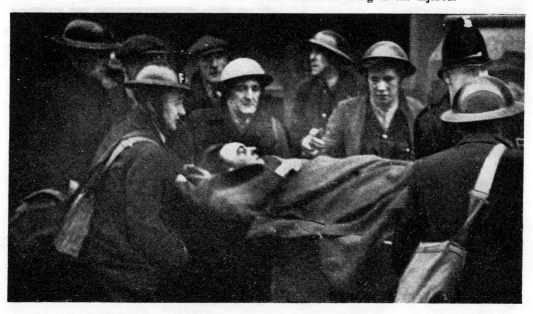

the other Services. The Rescue Squads were fully extended. Of the parties coming in from outside, one—from Hoylake—was hit by a high explosive bomb and all its members were killed or severely injured.

Great damage was done to property. A very large proportion of the private dwelling-houses in this mainly residential and dormitory Borough were rendered uninhabitable. Eleven churches were hit, the electricity works at Poulton, both the gas-holders were rendered useless. The pumping station at Seaview received a direct hit. So also at Birkenhead. There were many fires, a great many people trapped presenting a large scale rescue problem, many people killed and injured.

Roads blocked by craters and debris hindered the operations of our Services and added to the difficulties and dangers. At Bebington, also, many people were killed. Nor did Liverpool escape. Fire destroyed the upper storeys of the General Post Office.

But the three nights passed and again there was a pause in the attack. Once again the work of restoration was organised ; Military and Home Guard assistance was brought in ; hundreds of workmen were mobilised ; grabs, bull-dozers, cranes and transport were concentrated on the task of restoring Mersey-side once again to the full strength of its war effort. And the people braced themselves and carried on with their jobs.

So did the people of Merseyside await without dismay the next attack.

At 10.50 on the night of the 1st May, 1941, it came, when the first bomb was dropped on Wallasey. Within a very few minutes, high explosive bombs, incendiaries, and flares, were falling. It was the commencement of an attack more severe in its weight, its con-centration, and its continuity than had been experienced by any other area except London, and more severe perhaps in its concentration than even London had experienced.

It was the enemy's most desperate attempt to destroy the Port of Liverpool, partly by actual destruction of the great docks them-selves, partly by breaking the morale of the people without whom the Docks could not function. It failed.

The main weight of the attack fell on Bootle and on Liverpool. At Bootle, a large number of the houses in the town were rendered uninhabitable. An Emergency Rest Centre was hit ; twelve brave women of the W.V.S. engaged in preparing meals for the homeless were themselves killed. The fires were enormous.

DAY and night the Rescue Parties search for victims.

THE FRIENDLY HAND.—These heroic Merseysiders, bombed out but undaunted, at least don't go hungry, thanks to the Food Lorry from America.

On the 3rd May, in Liverpool and Birkenhead together, there were several hundred separate incidents and hundreds of fires requiring attention.

On the night of the 5th-6th, some 80 miles of hose, apart from a quantity of steel piping, were in use by the Fire Service.

On the night of the 7th-8th there were fires, " some very large," from Seaforth to the Huskisson Dock.

Between the 3rd and 10th May, 558 fire appliances were brought into the area from outside. Eighteen firemen were killed and 180 injured. At the request of the Regional Commissioner, an officer of great experience was brought in from London to take charge of the Fire Brigades throughout the Area.

Telephone communications were badly affected and Regional Headquarters and the Government Departments in Manchester were cut off and had to rely on wireless communication to mobile wireless stations in Liverpool.

Transport in the Northern and the middle part of the Docks and the centres of Bootle and Liverpool suffered particularly badly. Arrangements for traffic had to be improvised as best they could. In the Docks themselves several ships were sunk or gutted ; one was

SOUP AND SANDWICHES.— A Food Relief Convoy brings succour to blitzed Merseysiders.

'Removed to a new address.'

The writing on the . . . window.

Human Cameos

Little pictures with a big story

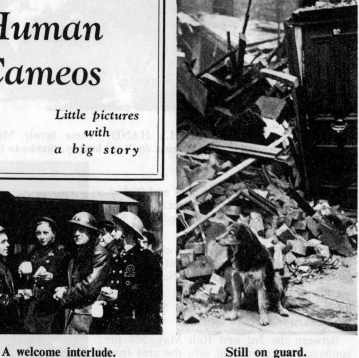

The bride's trousseau.

A welcome interlude.

Still on guard.

The Mersey smile.

All that is left . . . .

Not forgotten.

blown up, many were damaged ; traffic was gravely interrupted.

There was severe damage to the public utility services, and at one stage a complete interruption of the electricity supply.

The number of people rendered homeless was very large ; Liverpool alone dealt with 51,000 ; 75 per cent. of the Rest Centre accommodation at Bootle was destroyed ; hardly a house escaped damage. But improvised arrangements were hastily made. Churches, Church Halls, Cinemas, Schools, every kind of suitable building was pressed into use as Emergency Rest Centres. Very large numbers were billeted ; 10,000 blankets were rushed in ; the Military erected marquees and provided field kitchens. Mobile canteens were concentrated. In the result, it is believed that nobody went hungry. But Merseyside, battered, shaken, was not knocked out. Mr. Leslie, in his article, gives a detailed account of those terrible seven nights.

At 4.30 on the morning of the 8th May, the sirens sounded the all clear again. For all the people knew the seventh raid would be followed that night by an eighth. And they went doggedly about their work to prepare for it. Rest Centres were cleared so as to make room for more homeless ; personnel of the Civil Defence Services were relieved ; fresh reinforcements were brought in.

All day the fires were fought ; more emergency water supplies were provided ; Military, Civil Defence personnel and civilians worked feverishly to demolish dangerous buildings, clear the streets and prepare as far as might be for the battle of the coming night.

Everything was concentrated on repairing the damage of the last and on getting ready to take the next blow. But there was no next blow. The enemy had exhausted himself before he exhausted Merseyside. There was some scattered raiding at Bootle—but the attack was over, and Merseyside, backed up by all the resources of the Region, had won.

It was many days before the normal life of the great port could be re-established. But at once the work of reconstruction began. Heavy clearance was dealt with at first by the Military, and steps were taken to call in civilian labour ; on the day of the last raid, the whole of the Military on this work were replaced by civilians brought in by the Regional Emergency Works organisation.

By the 9th May, some 6,000 or 7,000 workmen had been sent into the area, and repairs to damaged factories and to damaged homes were proceeding apace.

Within a few days, Merseyside had got its breath back. By the end of the month, the Port was within reach of its previous efficiency, the telephone service had been largely restored, public utilities were almost back to normal, and clearance of essential roads was practically complete. Railways were still affected within the City, but a large volume of traffic was being handled. Of the factories which had been damaged, a very large number were again in full production. Merseyside was back at work. And with a greater sense of urgency than ever before.

In all, Merseyside has had 68 raids ; in Liverpool, Birkenhead, Bootle, and Wallasey, 3,966 people were killed ; 3,812 seriously injured. The last time that bombs fell on Merseyside was on the 10th January, 1942. They may never fall again. But the Civil Defence Services, started by those men and women who in 1937 commenced to prepare against the possible danger ahead, will not allow their efficiency or their keenness to be diminished by that possibility. Always there is the danger that the enemy may adopt new methods or turn to a different strategy of attack.

So long as the German Air Force remains in being—and depleted and discredited though it largely is—it remains still a powerful weapon of war, so long must we remain prepared for its attacks.

It is a dull business, this waiting, this standing by. But just as the original members of the Services prepared themselves in 1937 and 1938, just as the Services stood by from September, 1939, to those first raids in July and August, 1940, so now they remain on guard against the possibility of desperate attack by a desperate enemy. And so the Civil Defence Services on Merseyside remain, upholding to the full the great traditions which they have established. The personnel have reason to be proud of their Services— and Merseyside is proud of them.

The Attack on the Churches

By W. Innes Hutchison

ECCLESIASTICAL properties on Merseyside have suffered very severely from enemy air raids, and reconstruction and repair constitute one of the great problems by which the Churches are faced.

Where it has been practicable, damaged buildings have been made good, but this touches only the fringe of the devastation, and not until the war is over can anything greater be attempted. Meanwhile the situation is the subject of concentrated consideration on the part of the denominations, the desire being to plan in the best possible way for post-war conditions, so that, under the blessedness of peace, the Church may exert all its influence on the side of religious revival and social improvement.

The cost of the raids to the churches, measured in monetary terms, has been enormous, and the restriction and dislocation of their work and the disintegrating effect on congregational life have been a saddening experience. But there have been compensations, not the least of which has been the achievement of a greater inter-denominational unity, and a readiness by churches that have escaped suffering to help those not so fortunate.

Tribute has been paid to the courage and fortitude of the people of Merseyside during every blitz. These virtues were never more strikingly revealed than during the terrible raids at the beginning of May, 1941. Some churches had suffered prior to this period, but it was the enemy visitation in the month named that wrought the greatest devastation. All over the area places of worship were crushed into rubble, or reduced to gaunt skeletons by the onrush of fire.

Yet amid these appalling scenes church-

St. Luke's Church, Liverpool—as it was known all over the world.

After the wings of the vandal had passed. The spectacle from the altar.

going people did not lose heart. Their beloved church may have been smashed or marred, but it would live again in the better days ahead. This was the spirit by which their people were animated. Those days may tarry, but they are awaited in faith and confidence, and this attitude of the laity to great disaster is a source of strength to those on whom the heavy burden of reconstruction and replanning has fallen.

Church of England Losses

Liverpool Cathedral suffered badly. Outwardly the damage was not so distressingly apparent as in the case of many parish churches, although it was bad enough, but a look round the interior revealed a stretch of havoc, especially to stained glass windows, which suffered from bomb-blast. The wreck of so much valuable glass means a great outlay on restoration, but the Cathedral Committee lost no time in ordering new windows, and when peace comes the Cathedral's wounds will be healed.

There was widespread regret at the destruction of Liverpool's parish church, St. Nicholas', Pier Head. All that remained of this centuries-old landmark on the water front is the tower and spire and a vestry and blackened, fire-scorched walls. Great relief was felt when the Bishop announced that this venerable church will be rebuilt, and in the meantime the services are conducted in a temporary building on the vacant space bounded by the charred walls.

Another serious loss was St. Luke's, Bold Street. Nave and chancel went but the commanding tower still dominates the locality. It remains to be seen whether this church will be rebuilt. St. Michael's, Pitt Street, and the fine parish church of Walton were also destroyed.

Among churches seriously damaged is that of Mossley Hill. This was one of the first in the diocese to be struck. This occurred in the summer of 1940, when much stone work was smashed, and other wreckage caused.

Figures can never tell the whole tale, and, significant as they are in connection with this matter of mere destruction, their real value lies in emphasising the vastness of the problem committed to those in all the denominations on whom rests the responsibility of rebuilding

Another beloved Merseyside church, St. Nicholas' Parish Church, Liverpool, after the blitz, and (below) the tiny temporary church built this year within the ruins.

and restoration. Take, for instance, the Church of England. Details gathered by the Liverpool Diocesan Secretary, (Archdeacon C. F. Twitchett), show that in the diocese of Liverpool, of which Merseyside forms a large part, 100 churches were badly damaged, of which 17 were a total loss ; 6 of 68 vicarages were completely destroyed ; 6 church halls have been lost out of 54 damaged ; 47 schools were affected, and 6 of them were a total loss, while 32 other properties were more or less knocked about. These included the Church House in South John Street, which was completely wrecked. The value of demolished and damaged buildings is estimated at £750,000.

Heavy losses were also sustained in Birkenhead and Wallasey, which are in the diocese of Chester. But here, as elsewhere, clergy and Free Church ministers carried on their services, thanks to a very helpful spirit of co-operation between congregations, churches that had escaped scars welcoming worshippers of less fortunate places. In Wallasey no Anglican churches were completely destroyed, but some of them were damaged extensively, these including St. Luke's, Poulton and St. John's, Egremont. In Birkenhead among the churches damaged were St. Saviour's, Oxton, St. Ann's (near Park Station), St. Michael's, Claughton, and St. Peter's, Rock Ferry.

The Free Churches

The enemy took heavy toll of the Free Churches of Merseyside. The list of destroyed churches includes the Hamlet Free Church in Aigburth Road, and Kirkdale Tabernacle, the Welsh Congregational Churches in Marsh Lane, Kensington, Great Mersey Street, and Vittoria Street, Birkenhead, the English Presbyterian church of Mount Pleasant, St. Paul's, Bootle, and Trinity, Orrell, and the churches in Fitzclarence Street and Stanley Road of the Presbyterian Church of Wales. The Methodists lost Zion Church, Northumberland Terrace, Laird Street Church, Birkenhead, and churches in Wallasey hit were those in Poulton Road and Rowson Street. The Unitarian church in Bessborough Road, Birkenhead, was destroyed.

A HALLOWED MEMORY.— The ruins of St. Catherine's Church, Liverpool, associated with 'Woodbine Willie,' the late Rev. Studdert Kennedy.

Roman Catholic

The Roman Catholic Church was also a heavy sufferer on Merseyside. She lost places of worship and properties attached to them on both sides of the river, besides damage, in many cases extensive, to other centres of work. Like the other denominations, Archbishop Downey and those immediately associated with him had to plan quickly to meet so grave an emergency, to compute the loss in terms of money in readiness for the day when Government compensation will be forthcoming, and to bring order out of chaos, so that checks on the Church's work might be brought to the irreducible minimum.

Among the Liverpool churches destroyed were St. Mary's, Highfield Street, and Holy Cross, Great Crosshall Street ; also lost was St. Alexander's, Bootle. The badly damaged churches include that of The Blessed Sacrament, Aintree, and Our Lady Immaculate, St. Domingo Road.

Four large schools were total losses, these being St. Anne's, Edge Hill, St. Gerard's, Boundary Street, St. Alphonsus', Great Mersey Street, and St. Alexander's, Bootle. The damage done in the Archdiocese is estimated at £420,000, and nearly all this applies to Merseyside, excluding properties on the Cheshire side of the river belonging to the Shrewsbury diocese.

In New Brighton the Church in Hope Street was practically destroyed, and in Birkenhead the church of Our Lady, North End, was demolished.

Other Sufferers

The Salvation Army suffered the total destruction of their buildings in Yate Street, Toxteth, and Salisbury Street, Birkenhead. Their property in Stanley Road, Bootle, was partially wrecked, and other buildings were slightly damaged, these being in Walton Road, Poulton Road, Seacombe, Utting Avenue, Liverpool, Denton Street, Dingle, and Clifton Street, Everton.

Some of the unattached centres of religious work also suffered. The hall in Liverpool where the Rev. W. Barrow-Williams conducted his mission was demolished, and Stanley Park church, of which the Rev. T. B. Wilmot is the minister, lost its windows, and its vestries in Fountains Road were badly damaged.

At the Cathedral, where the Derby Memorial was damaged.

Hamlet Free Church, Aigburth, after being struck by an oil bomb.

❖

SCENE OF TRAGEDY.
The damage at Our Lady's Church, Birkenhead, where a direct hit on his Presbytery killed Canon Tallon.

❖

AIR WAR OVER LIVERPOOL —I SHOOT DOWN A HEINKEL

By Flying Officer R. M. R. Baldock

DURING May, 1941, Liverpool and the Merseyside were taking all the Hun had to offer, and his offerings were by no means meagre.

Apart from the valuable work of the A.A. defences, the defence of Merseyside was entrusted to squadrons of night-fighters equipped with " Defiants "—the stubby two-seater with crew consisting of pilot and air gunner. My squadron was stationed some miles north of Liverpool.

As soon as darkness falls crews are at two stages of readiness—Immediate and Thirty minutes. Men on Immediate are to be found at Dispersal sprawled about and entertaining themselves in their own various ways.

One evening, during the month of May, 1941, which no resident of Merseyside will forget—" A " flight Dispersal had its usual flock of aircrew hanging around. In one corner was congregated a little poker school in which were my pilot and myself. There were Don and Hutch ; a year later they " bought it " on an op. over the Irish Sea. There were Pete and his gunner, Joe. Pete was killed six months ago when his Beaufighter crashed, but Joe was lucky and is back on ops. The third pair was Johnny and myself.

Johnny and I were at Readiness and the time was 21.30. The game had been going well for everyone except me. I hadn't had anything better than three Aces the whole night.

But this hand was different. Four lovely fat Queens. Six fair-sized piles of odd silver were ranged around the table but I knew that my four Queens would beat all other hands. A pleasant vision of a party later loomed up.

Then, from the Flight Commander in the next room came : " Get Cracking—Flap ! "

Johnny and I grabbed our small heaps of money and rushed for the door out into the dark. The aircraft was already out of its bay, standing with the engine running. I put myself in the rear cockpit of our Diffy.

Soon we were moving along the perimeter, shortly to swing into the runway.

" Purler 12 calling Control. Scramble ? " called Johnny on the radio telephone.

" Purler 12 O.K. Scramble." came back Control.

" All Set, Stiffy ? " yelled Johnny.

" Let's go," I replied.

We made off for the South at full throttle.

" Hello Control—Purler 12—Airborne— Listening Out."

As we were making off South, gaining height rapidly, the voice of Sector Ops., came through : " Hello Purler 12—Donner Control—Bandit South West Sector Angels 12, Vector 220."

Within what seemed a very little time we were at the required position and Sector ordered us to turn on vector 090 and keep sharp look-out. This is always the time when the tummy gives that funny rising feeling and the hairs on the back of the neck seem to stand up.

However, it all stops when the Hun is sighted. Then a cold stillness settles on you.

We were now both peering out into the darkness, each hoping to be the first to spot the bandit.

It is common knowledge that the term used in Fighter Command to indicate the presence of the Hun is that old English hunting expression " Tally Ho ! " My own pilot, I regret to say, has his own strange manner of expressing his delight on sighting the Hun. This is not only unprintable but also unmentionable.

Our luck was in. Silhouetted against the background of cumulus was a lovely fat Heinkel III. Quietly (if you can so describe the shocking noise the Diffy makes) we crept up on him. So far so good. No red pinpoints from his aircraft to suggest that he was throwing muck at us.

It seemed a long time, but eventually,

there he was, as big as a house. Johnny had placed him in just the right spot.

"Easy now," I remember saying to myself, "Not much deflection. Don't get excited. Short bursts."

"Let him have it, Stiffy. Even *you* can't miss." Johnny's voice came over the inter-com.

Much harder than necessary, I pressed the button. Thank God! I had it on FIRE and not SAFE as I had done once before. Into the port engine of the Hun I could see the odd tracers thrusting. Just a two-second burst (mustn't jam guns) and repeat the dose. A glow from his engine as I released the pressure, and then once more as he turned gently over on his starboard side. No calmness now. He was alight—now to finish him off. A long burst and down he went like a meteor, leaving a red and orange trail that stopped when he hit the water.

"Nice work, Stiffy. I knew you could hit a pig in a passage," said Johnny.

We chattered over the inter-com . . .

"Let's go home—Supper time."

"Know where we are? Or shall we pretend that we do and request a confirming vector from Control?" asked Johnny.

THE KILL. An artist's impression of a duel between a night-fighter and a Heinkel III.

"Beacon at two o'clock. Let's go look-see. Probably Base."

As we neared the beacon its flashes winked at us: Dah, Dah, Dah—Dah, Di, Dah. O.K. in code.

"That's us," I said. "We are coded Orange King to-night."

"O.K. I should jolly-well think so—let's get in."

As we went round the circuit we called on the radio telephone for permission to land. Control gave us the O.K. and as we made the final run-in Johnny called for "floods," and on came the lights flooding the runway with light brighter than day.

Johnny set her down gently. The flood-lights were switched off as soon as the Controller saw that we were down, and we turned off at the intersection of the runway and taxied off to Dispersal.

As soon as the engine was switched off the ground crew were around us with their questions.

"Any luck, Sergeant?"

"Heinkel . . . Flames . . . In the drink."

"Good show."

Having assured the fitters and armourers of the good working of the aircraft—the result of their work—we shot off to the crew room and the ground crew were left content, no doubt, to prepare a bigger line to shoot than the one we had in mind.

Back in the crew room we gave the "gen." to the I.O. (Intelligence Officer) and the blokes suggested supper. My eyes wandered to the table where the cards were lying as we had left them.

"Come on—let's finish the game," I urged.

"Got something good, Stiffy."

"Not too good," I lied.

"Supper" was the cry.

I tried to insist, but they wouldn't have it.

"What had you got, Stiffy?" asked Johnny.

"Four fat Queens and I should have picked up a packet."

"What are you binding at? You got a Heinkel, didn't you?"

That's all there is of that—but we gathered later that that Hun we got was fully loaded and was not a returned empty. So a load of rubbish that was meant for someone in Liverpool finished in the drink.

But—that was a lovely hand of Four Queens!

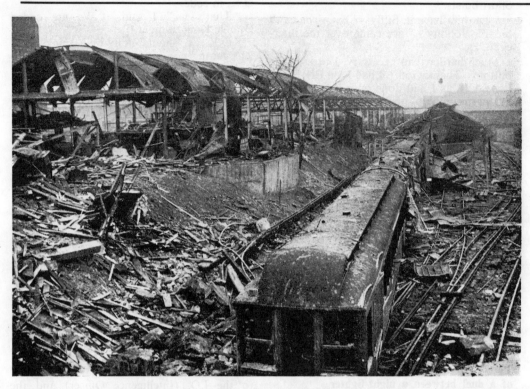

❖

Park Station,
Birkenhead,
blitzed heavily
(above), and
(right), as it is
today with
barely a sign
of damage.

❖

Barrowmore Hall, near Chester, home of the East Lancashire Tuberculosis Colony, blitzed in November, 1940, and (below) the modern new Sanatorium.

A PAGE OF BLITZ FACTS

During the early morning of July 29, 1940 (about the same time that bombs dropped harmlessly in fields about Thurstaston, Irby and Neston) a few bombs fell near a searchlight site at Altcar without doing any serious damage.

On August 1, in the early morning, a few bombs dropped at Halewood, one of them disturbing a number of tombstones in a graveyard, while another dropped in a field.

In the early morning of August 9, about half an hour after midnight, a stick of H.E.'s fell at Birkenhead, one of them hitting Mr. Bunney's house at Prenton, where a servant girl was killed.

Twenty-four hours later, in the early morning of August 10 (again about half an hour after midnight), seven H.E.'s dropped at Wallasey, when property was damaged, four people were killed and four seriously injured. The total casualties were thirty-two in that first raid on Wallasey.

Liverpool had its first bombs around midnight on August 17 (Saturday). They fell in the Caryl Street area. There was damage to the Overhead Railway and a shed, but a block of tenements was undamaged by a bomb which made a big crater in the roadway nearby.

* * * *

120,000 houses were damaged in Liverpool.

* * * *

A word of praise is due to Liverpool Emergency Committee who were given considerable war-time administrative powers by the City Council and who, since the war started, have met regularly—at one period, as frequently as three times a day—to keep a watchful eye on the city's affairs. To them must go a large share of the credit for Liverpool's remarkable recovery from enemy attacks.

Similar patriotism and devotion to duty has been shown in all other parts of Merseyside by civic leaders who were given special powers in the control of local administration.

THE TOLL: A Month by Month Record

LIVERPOOL.

	Killed.	Seriously Injured.
AUGUST, 1940	37	73
SEPTEMBER, 1940	221	357
OCTOBER, 1940	106	90
NOVEMBER, 1940	305	192
DECEMBER, 1940	412	382
JANUARY, 1941	43	23
FEBRUARY, 1941	2	7
MARCH, 1941	101	99
APRIL, 1941	36	105
MAY, 1941	1,453	1,065

WALLASEY.

	Killed.	Seriously Injured.
AUGUST, 1940	9	10
SEPTEMBER, 1940	4	2
OCTOBER, 1940	3	3
NOVEMBER, 1940	3	3
DECEMBER, 1940	119	91
JANUARY, 1941	2	3
FEBRUARY, 1941	—	—
MARCH, 1941	189	158
APRIL, 1941	—	—
MAY, 1941	3	19

BIRKENHEAD.

	Killed.	Seriously Injured.
AUGUST, 1940	4	23
SEPTEMBER, 1940	24	65
OCTOBER, 1940	17	56
NOVEMBER, 1940	2	3
DECEMBER, 1940	63	105
JANUARY, 1941	8	15
FEBRUARY, 1941	—	—
MARCH, 1941	228	275
APRIL, 1941	8	20
MAY, 1941	28	44

BOOTLE.

	Killed.	Seriously Injured.
AUGUST, 1940	—	—
SEPTEMBER, 1940	28	60
OCTOBER, 1940	10	18
NOVEMBER, 1940	6	4
DECEMBER, 1940	108	93
JANUARY, 1941	—	—
FEBRUARY, 1941	—	—
MARCH, 1941	—	—
APRIL, 1941	—	—
MAY, 1941	257	26

+ 5 missing